Between Rock and a Hard Place

More Cartoons by Pat Oliphant

Andrews, McMeel & Parker
A Universal Press Syndicate Affiliate
Kansas City • New York

Foreword

People believe that because what Pat Oliphant does is called political *cartooning*, he's poking fun at things. Fact of the matter he's not: He's deadly serious. Fact of the matter is he's a mean SOB who has been endowed with the sort of glorious sense of outrage we all should have when we see the self-important panjandrums in control of this planet running amok. Fact of the matter is, we should all be out there on the barricades with Oliphant, screaming that we're mad as hell and we're not gonna take it anymore.

Oliphant doesn't take it anymore. And we're all the richer for it.

What I like best about him is the way he gives it to everybody. Some of my more self-righteous Jewish friends think he's anti-Semitic because of the way he stuck it to Menachem Begin and Ariel Sharon during the Israeli invasion of Lebanon back in 1982. (These are the kinds of people, I should add, who put "Shiksas Are for Practice" bumper stickers on their cars.) Oliphant doesn't hate Jews — there's not a prejudiced bone in his body. He simply has an abiding disgust for liars and cheats of every ethnic, racial, and national persuasion, including — small wonder — Israeli politicians who scream "Blood libel" when they're caught with their hands in the wrong cookie jar — or in 1982, the wrong Palestinian refugee camps.

He got in trouble with Italians for the way he treated the Zaccaros, too. You remember the Zaccaros — John and Geraldine. He's in real estate; she did a Pepsi commercial. Oliphant used a lot of "Whaddayou? Whaddayou?" dialect when he drew them. And people probably thought he had it in for everyone whose name ends in a vowel. He didn't: He only had it in for John and Geraldine. They probably deserved it.

In fact, Oliphant is one of the original proponents of equal rights. Liberals and conservatives, commies and capitalists, Democrats, Republicans, homosexuals, clerics (liberal-neoconservative-commie-homosexual clerics when he can find 'em) — you name it, he's skewered them all.

How he got so mean is a subject of some discussion. We who know and love him have decided that the root cause is the fact that he was born in Australia, and spent too many years upside down burbling, "Throw another shrimp on the barbie, mate," or some such rot.

These days he's doing his daily skewering in more than 500 newspapers, courtesy of Universal Press Syndicate. I wish we had Oliphant here in Washington on a daily basis. It would prevent us from taking ourselves too seriously. It would be an antidote to all the stuff we in the national press are writing about each other and about the inmates who are running the asylum.

We watch Dan Rather and Tom Brokaw and Peter Jennings and think we're getting the whole story. We're not. We sit in our living rooms watching the TV, getting blitzed with factoids and info-bits and visual wallpaper, and we're not screaming back at the screen as we should be. We're not outraged enough.

Thank God Pat Oliphant is.

— JOHN WEISMAN
Weisman is Washington, D.C., bureau chief of *TV Guide* magazine. His new novel, *Blood Cries*, will be published in May 1987.

'CAN YOU IMAGINE??! SELLING OUT THEIR COUNTRY FOR A FEW LOUSY BUCKS!!'

June 6, 1985

Spies, spies, spies . . .*

*This and all other postscripts by Pat Oliphant.

June 6, 1985

7

'HERE WE ARE, LIVE, WITH MR. ZEKE CRUMLIN, WHOSE ELDER HALF-SISTER WAS ONCE MARRIED TO A THIRD COUSIN OF ONE OF THE BEIRUT HOSTAGES... SIR, TELL US HOW YOU ARE COPING IN THIS CRISIS!'

TV, the Insatiable Beast

Robert Stethem, a hostage, was murdered by terrorists during a hijacking in Beirut.

MEANWHILE, AT A BOARD MEETING IN ATLANTA...

The president is operated on for colon cancer. TV takes you there.

July 17, 1985

'HEY, TERRIFIC—MAKING BOOK ON MY RECOVERY CHANCES—I'LL HAVE SOME OF THAT!'

16

'COULD YOU PLEASE GET BACK IN THE BOTTLE, SIR?'

A STATE OF EMERGENCY

'YOU MAY BE INTERESTED IN OUR THREE MILE ISLAND MODEL, PRESIDENT LI — IT COMES WITH AUTOMATIC POPULATION CONTROL.'

Chinese President Li shops for U.S. nuclear assistance.

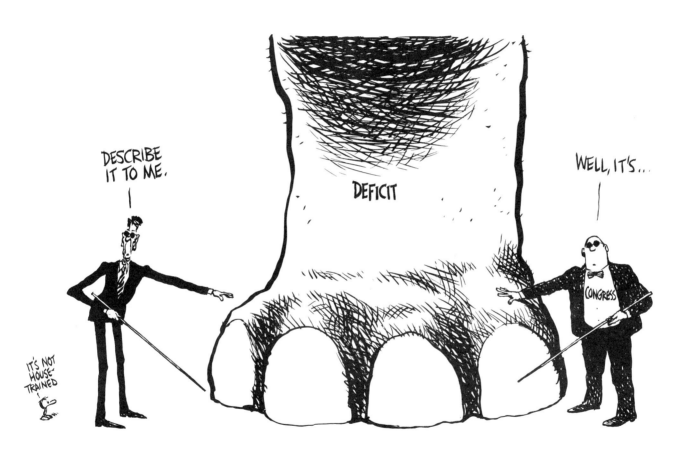

HOUNDED RELENTLESSLY ON APARTHEID BY THE REAGAN ADMINISTRATION, SOUTH AFRICA
HAS WITHDRAWN ITS AMBASSADOR TO THE U.S.

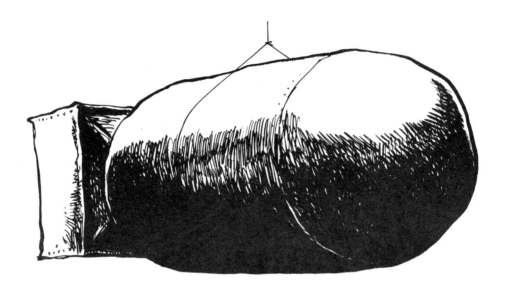

'ACTUALLY, AFTER FORTY YEARS, I RARELY GIVE IT A THOUGHT...'

An anniversary — The Bomb at 40

Blacks beat up on blacks in South Africa.

'THE INMATES ARE HAPPY, THE CONDITIONS ARE EXCELLENT, AND THE MAN IN CHARGE IS A VERY NICE GUY—AND A FINE CONSERVATIVE, I MIGHT ADD.'

August 28, 1985

ONE FINAL TEST BEFORE WE TALK...

"'FROM THE PRESIDENT OF THE UNITED STATES, GREETINGS'—I THINK YOU'VE BEEN DRAFTED.'

September 3, 1985

REAGAN WANTS ACCESS TO SOVIET TELEVISION.

RELIC

THE LADIES OF THE CLEAN MUSIC, QUILTING AND PORN WATCH SOCIETY DISCOVER YET ANOTHER DISGUSTING ROCK LYRIC.

French frogmen sink Greenpeace vessel in New Zealand. How much did Mitterrand know?

'PLEASED TO BE OF ASSISTANCE — AND NOW, MY BANKER WOULD LIKE TO TALK TO YOU ABOUT YOUR DELINQUENT MORTGAGE PAYMENTS.'

A disastrous earthquake in Mexico, and other ill-timed events.

'TELL HIM WE JUST WANT TO SING HIM SOME NICE SONGS ABOUT HARD TIMES DOWN ON THE FARM.'

October 1, 1985

56

'IMAGINE SEEING YOU UP HERE!'

For what must be the first time, Russian personnel are the victims of terrorism.

OUR POLICY BULLETIN BOARD

'SOME SUCKED-UP RUSSIAN TAPDANCER SAYS HE'S COME TO TAKE YOU AWAY FROM ALL THIS, MY DEAR.'

'.. WELCOME BACK, JUSTICE BURGER... HI, THERE, JUSTICE POWELL... GOOD DAY, JUSTICE MARSHALL... HELLO, JUSTICE BLACKMUN.. HELLO, JUSTICE FALWELL — JUSTICE FALWELL!!??'

THE OTHER APARTHEID

'IF I KNEW WHO WAS RESPONSIBLE, I WOULD PUNISH THEM MYSELF!'

'THIS HERE COURT FINDS YOU GUILTY AS CHARGED, WHICH YOU NO DOUBT, INDEED, PROBABLY ARE, OR YOU WOULDN'T BE HANGING AROUND LIKE THAT.

Egypt allows the Achille Lauro hijackers to escape.

'HIJACKED AN ITALIAN SHIP, MURDERED AN ELDERLY JEW IN A WHEELCHAIR, REINFORCED U.S.-ISRAELI RELATIONS, INCREASED THE CLIMATE OF VIOLENCE FURTHER... MY, MY, WHAT ELSE DID YOU DO TO US?'

'SORRY, LADIES—NO MORE AUTOGRAPHS TODAY. THE VICIOUS, UNFAIR HARDSHIPS OF HER TERRIBLE CAMPAIGN HAVE LEFT POOR MISS FERRARO FEELING QUITE DELICATE.'

AIDS SCARE BRINGS NEW GUILD RULINGS ON SCREEN KISSING—

November 6, 1985

SUDDENLY, INTUITIVELY, THE AWFUL REALIZATION HIT CIA AGENT BUMWORTHY—HIS DINNER COMPANION, THE RUSSIAN DEFECTOR, WOULD NOT BE COMING BACK!

The CIA loses a defector, who leaves a restaurant in D.C. to redefect to the Soviet Embassy.

THE SAGA CONTINUES — 3 REHABILITATED DEFECTORS EXCHANGE NOTES.

77

Redefectors, continued.

A royal visit to the U.S.

SOUTH AFRICA — THE AUTHORIZED VERSION.

'ASYLUM? WHAT ASYLUM? SPEAK ENGLISH, BOY—ALL I CAN HEAR IS GOBBLE GOBBLE GOBBLE!'

A Russian seaman attempting to defect is returned to his ship
by INS officers who can't understand him. Then came Thanksgiving . . .

'GOT HIM!'

Terrorist pursuit, Egyptian style

Israel spies on the U.S.

The Real President stands up.

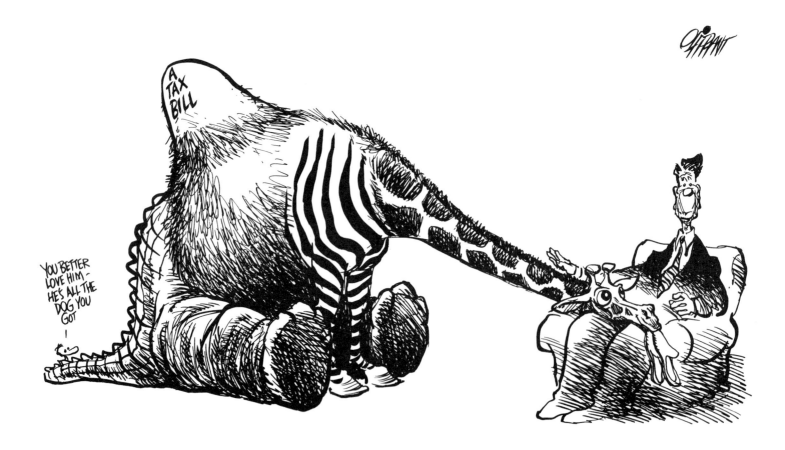

HAPPY SAKHAROV DISSIDENTS IN SALT MINE PICNIC SCENE — A KGB FILMS RELEASE

'WHY, HOWDY, GENERAL ... SURE, WE CAN FLY YOUR ARMY ANY PLACE ... WHY, YESSIR, WE DO UNDERSTAND YOU GOTTA CUT COSTS, SO WE'LL GIVE YOU PENTAGON BOYS A GOOD PRICE ...'

...AND BEHOLD, IT CAME TO PASS THAT THEY ALL WENT UP UNTO THE LAND OF THE SENATE.

JOSEPH CHECKS THE BILLS — AN APRÈS-CHRISTMAS TRADITION IS BORN...

'LORDY, I BARELY SLEPT A WINK — VISIONS OF SUGARPLUMS DANCED IN MY HEAD ALL NIGHT.'

Christmas morning in disadvantage-land

December 23, 1985

'WELCOME BACK, SIR. WHILE YOU WERE AWAY, OUR COMPANY ABSORBED YOUR COMPANY, MAKING YOU NOW PART OF MEGASIGMACORP, A SUBSIDIARY OF DYNAMAX WORLDWIDE, INC.'

Mergers, mergers . . .

Happy New Year!

'STEP OUT OF THE CAR, SIR.'

January 2, 1986

U.S. calls for sanctions against Libya in anti-terrorist move.

A ROSE
IS A ROSE
IS A ROSE

FALWELL'S
~~MORAL MAJORITY~~
LIBERTY
FEDERATION

AND BY ANY
OTHER NAME
SMELLS
JUST AS
MUCH

A national holiday is proclaimed for Dr. Martin Luther King, Jr.

NETWORKS — THE DECISION PROCESS.

'HOW NICE TO GET BACK TO TRADITIONAL VALUES...'

'BANANAS? WHAT BANANAS??'

Little did we realize how many bananas the monkey had stolen.

The shuttle is lost.

January 29, 1986

ALARMED BY THE MANY DANGERS, THE PIONEERS ABANDONED WESTWARD EXPLORATION EXCEPT FOR A SERIES OF UNMANNED PRAIRIE PROBE VEHICLES...

Luckily, NASA wasn't in charge of the launch.

February 5, 1986

CONGRESS

ADMISSIONS

BUDGET

IS A TRAIN WRECK A CATASTROPHIC ILLNESS?

'ARE YOU COVERED BY CATASTROPHIC ILLNESS INSURANCE?'

C'mon listen — the man's serious.

Philippine election time

RAMBITO

February 21, 1986

Marcos claims election victory.

Done and done.

'PERSONALLY, I MUCH PREFERRED THE OLD LECTURE ABOUT THE INVINCIBLE INFALLIBILITY OF OUR SUPERIOR SYSTEM.'

Gorbachev moves to get Russia moving again.

'SIR, THIS IS NOT A SAFE AREA FOR YOU TO BE IN. PLEASE ALLOW ME TO HAND YOUR MONEY TO THIS UNIFORMED OFFICER FOR SAFE-KEEPING.'

March 3, 1986

Asylum for a dictator yearning to breathe free.

ONWARD! AND DOWNWARD

On the move again

Lawyers, torts, insurance companies, premiums, big settlements, lawyers, torts, etc. . . .

Secrets from Imelda's closet

March 20, 1986

The Marcoses search for a suitable permanent home.

March 25, 1986

LET A THOUSAND FLOWERS BLOOM.

U.S. bombs Libya.

No aid for the Nicaraguan Contras.

Then, Ortega attacks the Contras in Honduras . . .

Easter again.

In Illinois, rabid right winger Lyndon LaRouche successfully launches
his own Democratic candidates for lieutenant governor and secretary of state.

April 1, 1986

'HELLO? HEY, WHAT'S HAPPENIN', MOAMMAR, BABY? WHY, SURE I CAN GET HIM TO TALK TO YOU — MIKE GORBACHEV JUST CALLED TO ASK THE SAME THING. HOW MUCH?'

Deaver left the White House and went into business for himself.

More terrorism

"'SCUSE ME — WHERE WOULD YOU FOLKS LIKE YOUR RADIO-ACTIVE WASTE?'"

Coming, ready or not.

BUSH OF ARABIA.

ALLIES.

The Gadhafi dilemma

Pity the poor IRS.

The Stockman book goes on the market.

'LET ME POINT OUT THAT IN THE UNITED STATES THIS HAPPENS ALL THE TIME!'

Meltdown at Chernobyl

Please! Not in polite society!

More on David Stockman, recent millionaire

The Titan explodes at launch.

May 7, 1986

The Summit in Japan

Kurt Waldheim, the Austrian people's choice.

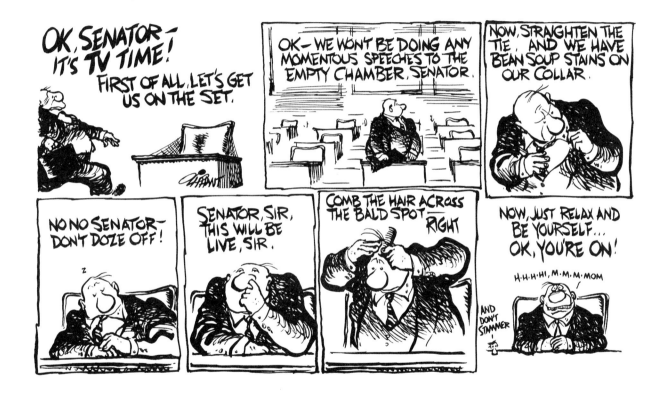

Senate on TV for the first time

ROVER, A 24 GRAND-A-YEAR, LOW LEVEL WATCHDOG, WAS LEFT IN CHARGE OF A MILLION DOLLAR STEAK. BAD DOG, ROVER!

CONGRESSIONAL ARAB-BASHING

May 22, 1986

The opening of the Silly Season